Live Life on Purpose

Live Life on Purpose

ADAM DURAN

Copyright © 2022 by Adam Duran
Live Life on purpose

All rights reserved. No part of this publication may be reproduced, distributed or transmitted in any form or by any means, including photocopying, recording, or other electronic or mechanical methods, without the prior written permission of the publisher, except in the case of brief quotations embodied in critical reviews and certain other non-commercial uses permitted by copyright law.

Although the author and publisher have made every effort to ensure that the information in this book was correct at press time, the author and publisher do not assume and hereby disclaim any liability to any party for any loss, damage, or disruption caused by errors or omissions, whether such errors or omissions result from negligence, accident, or any other cause.

Adherence to all applicable laws and regulations, including international, federal, state and local governing professional licensing, business practices, advertising, and all other aspects of doing business in the US, Canada or any other jurisdiction is the sole responsibility of the reader and consumer.

Neither the author nor the publisher assumes any responsibility or liability whatsoever on behalf of the consumer or reader of this material. Any perceived slight of any individual or organization is purely unintentional.

The resources in this book are provided for informational purposes only and should not be used to replace the specialized training and professional judgment of a health care or mental health care professional.

Neither the author nor the publisher can be held responsible for the use of the information provided within this book. Please always consult a trained professional before making any decision regarding treatment of yourself or others.

CONTENTS

INTRODUCTION	9
1. PAST IS PROLOGUE	13
2. MY YOUNGER YEARS	21
3. MY HIGH SCHOOL YEARS	27
4. HIGHER PURPOSE	33
5. COLLEGE YEARS	37
6. GETTING MARRIED	43
7. DON'T GIVE UP	71
8. TROUBLE IN PARADISE	75
9. CONTROL YOUR ATTITUDE	83
10. CHALLENGING YOURSELF	93

11. ASSOCIATIONS ON PURPOSE AND
    OTHER GOOD HABITS   101

12. GENEROSITY   109

CONCLUSION   113

ACKNOWLEDGEMENTS   121

LIVE LIFE ON PURPOSE
By
Adam Duran

This book is dedicated to my late father, John Tinoco Duran. Your decision to follow Jesus gave our family purpose. Thank you.

INTRODUCTION

A long time ago, I made it a daily habit to read about how other people succeeded in life, whether it was professionally, personally, physically, emotionally, financially, or spiritually. I incorporated the tools and techniques in my life that I learned, and others around me began to notice how well these healthy habits worked for me. So, if you incorporate the habits outlined in this book, they can change your life for the better and help those around you! If no one has ever told you before, YOU matter, and WHAT you do matters! I CARE about YOU, YOU are LOVED, and I want this book to positively impact your life. I also don't want this just for you. If this works for you, which I know it will, please share it with others so that it can impact the WORLD!

If someone told my younger self that I would grow up to lead a disciplined lifestyle, have an accomplished nearly 30-year career as a law enforcement officer, be a Boston Marathon qualifier four years in a row, and that my story would be an inspiration to others, I would have looked over my shoulder and wondered who the heck they were talking to. Truth be told, growing up, I was a kid who lacked focus and who was a bit of a troublemaker. My future was never something I put any real thought into. I learned not to let my past define my future. I learned to believe that God has a plan for everyone, however, we must realize that and know that ceilings are manmade and that the sky's the limit on what we can accomplish! I learned that effective daily habits and commitments can be fuel for long-term success. It is worth repeating that the changes I made in my life did not happen overnight or by chance, but by choice. They were the result of time, effort, and studying with purpose the tools and techniques required for success. Then, it was only a matter of learning how to discipline myself to be intentional about what I wanted and to truly 'Live Life on Purpose.'

My purpose in writing this book is to help you find your purpose and to set a goal which you will need in fulfilling that purpose. Finding your purpose and developing a plan will excite and drive you. Once someone realizes and believes they have purpose, they can finally start to take action by controlling their thought pattern. When action is taken with a "no quit" attitude, one's dreams can and will be realized. You are limitless and unstoppable if you believe you are! There is a quote from Henry Ford that says, "Whether you think you can, or you think you can't—you're right." This emphasizes how a positive mental attitude can quickly impact the difference between success and failure. Your attitude will determine your altitude, meaning how high you go in life is determined by a positive mental mindset. Whether you are in a good place or feeling a bit unmotivated about your future, if you use some of the tips and techniques I lay out in this book which have helped me, I know they will also help you achieve your goals and dreams. I never felt that I was the smartest nor the most talented, but the one thing I came to realize was if I was willing to put in the kind of time and effort, I would be able to outwork many people. If you get started at working towards a goal and are willing to work hard at it, one of three things will happen: You will come close to hitting your goal, hit your goal, or even possibly surpass your goal! So, if you're ready to begin taking your life to a higher level, put your seatbelts on and keep reading!

1

PAST IS PROLOGUE

You may not have started out being your best, but that doesn't mean you can't turn out to be your best. Whether it's because of your family, surroundings, or your inner belief, you might not see a bigger picture for yourself. By not seeing more for ourselves, we prevent ourselves from living up to our full potential, which is ultimately disempowering for us.

I look back to February of 2015 as a perfect example of how far I have come from where I started. I received a phone call from the Sheriff and her executive management team. They were calling to inform me that I was being promoted to the rank of Correctional Sergeant. To say I was happy to get that phone call would be an understatement. While the call was brief, the journey to get that call was long. I get emotional even today when I think about it. After I thanked the Sheriff and the executive management team for the great news, I called my dad. He started crying after I told him what I had accomplished and he said, "I'm proud of you." My dad loved me, but was never a real "touchy feely" kind of dad. I had not heard these words from him too often before, so hearing them in that moment meant the world to me.

The promotional ceremony was held in April at our Sheriff's Department headquarters. Many family members and friends of those who were promoted were in attendance at the auditorium. Most of the sheriff's department executive management team were also there. Many family members of mine had shown up, so to say this was a very special day for me was an understatement.

All those who were being promoted were called up one by one. They were called up alphabetically and identified by name, their accomplishments, and the rank they were being promoted to. Some people, like myself, were being promoted to sergeant, and others to lieutenant or captain. Since my last name was "Duran," I was the second or third sergeant called up. I was dressed in my sheriff's office class A uniform with an Ike jacket. My Ike jacket at the time had four hash marks on my left sleeve (each hash mark indicates five years of service), showing I had served at least twenty years in the department. My Ike jacket also had chevron stripes on the upper part of either arm, indicating the rank of sergeant. When my name was called to walk up to the stage and officially receive my promotion, I walked over to where my dad was sitting, took him by his arm and assisted him up to the front of the auditorium. He had to walk with a cane at this point of his life due to a stroke he had suffered years before.

As I was presented with a sergeant's badge by the sheriff, my dad helped pin it on me. The pride he had expressed to me on that phone call a couple of months earlier had not gone anywhere. At that moment, I went back in time. In my younger years I lacked confidence in myself, and seldom felt confident and validated in my career or other aspects in my life. This very moment gave me a boost in confidence that helped me gain a sense of validation and recognition that the choices I was making, books I was reading, and my associations were helping me reach my highest potential. This moment, which was made possible by many moments that came before it. As I mentioned before, this boosted my confidence and self-esteem. I hadn't felt that way too often before, and now I started thinking maybe I could reach for higher goals. I have realized that people, events, and situations can really have a positive or negative affect on our lives. The kid who had been called a quitter, who had gotten into his share of trouble with the law, and was a high school dropout was now Sergeant Adam Duran. I began to reflect on my life, looking back at how I got here.

Although my family were hard workers and wanted nothing but the best for me, nothing about my family history suggested that I was going to be handed success on a silver platter. My mother, Hope Cervantez, was born and raised in San Jose, California. Despite my mom's sunny mood, she grew up in a very difficult household.

My father, John Tinoco Duran, was from Delano, California and moved to San Jose around 1961. My dad also grew up in a difficult home environment. He was an 'old school' disciplinarian with a no-nonsense type of attitude.

When my parents met, my dad was nineteen and my mom was fifteen. My dad had just moved to San Jose from Delano. They married when my mom was just sixteen. Since my mom's home life was so difficult, getting married was a way for her to get out of the house. By the time my mom was nineteen, she was married with three kids; my older brother, Johnny, my older sister, Stephanie; and then finally, me.

My dad served a short stint in the military before I was born. He went to boot camp at Fort Sill in Oklahoma and then was stationed at Fort Ord near Monterey, California for less than a year. My mom had such a rough time raising two babies on her own that my dad was able to get an early honorable discharge from the military due to family hardship. He started working in the post office in 1964. He was a special delivery mailman who would deliver packages all over the city, even on Christmas Day, long before Amazon or FedEx even existed.

I grew up in East San Jose. At that time, each neighborhood on that side of town tended to be very territorial with its own neighborhood gangs. While I had a good home, my neighborhood was considered to be in the rougher part of town. Many of the kids just hung out and got into trouble via fighting and other means. My childhood home was somewhat of a party house. We had a fully stocked wet bar in the house and a pool table in the garage. We would frequently have parties there on Friday and Saturday nights. My dad rode motorcycles, so we often had many bikers come to the house to play pool and party. I'll never forget some of their nicknames. There was this guy named Tom, but they called him Midnight, and his brother was called Quarter to Twelve. They were called those names because of their dark complexion. Another guy's name was Physical Ed because he was a bodybuilder. While my dad wasn't a full-patched member of any motorcycle club, there were a few guys who were, and they would ride over to our house to join in the various parties that we would host. My dad rode a 1967 Harley Davidson Electra Glide 1200. Due to lots of heavy drinking, fights would occasionally occur during these parties. My dad was never one to shy away from a fight. It probably didn't hurt that he carried a dagger in a leather sheath on the right side of his hip in plain view, which, as I can remember, was about ten inches long. My dad could be a bit hot-tempered at times, and he was known to throw punches first and ask questions later.

My brother, sister, and I learned how to play pool at a very young age. My dad taught us, and we all got pretty good at it. I even had my own personal pool cue. We would practice playing pool almost daily. My dad would also take us for rides on his Harley, but he never wanted us to own one for ourselves. Even though my dad never once wore a helmet he would tell us that motorcycles were just too dangerous. After work and on weekends, my dad would often ride off to his favorite bar to go hang out with his friends. I think my mom was happy when he was at home having the parties because she would rather have him home than at the bar. My mom worked outside the home and worked the night shift so she could be there for us as much as she could when we got up before and after school. She would say that as long as she had her children, she didn't need much else.

My brother Johnny has always had a good head on his shoulders. He's always been athletic and knew what he wanted out of life, and was disciplined enough to go after what he wanted. My brother was very mature and always tried to steer my sister and I in the right direction. My sister Stephanie was also athletic, with a good head on her shoulders. She knew I was a bit of a wild child, and she and her boyfriend Eddie, who later became her husband, looked after me even when I wasn't necessarily doing the right thing. I was the one in the family who you had to keep any eye on. I had menace tendencies. I had a lot of energy, and I became more mischievous as I got older. I was not as serious as my father and probably took more after my mother, who tended to be a bit more friendly. I liked to have a good time and was very outgoing. I was even voted friendliest in school. I have the strength of my father though, especially when I needed to take care of business. My dad had told me that I was never to start a fight, but if someone started one, I had to make sure I finished it. My dad's message to me was to never back down from a fight. My dad had a younger brother named David who also never backed down from a fight, and ended up with more than his share of trouble. I looked up to him. He had a big personality, a great smile, and was very athletic and muscular. He was that "cool" uncle to me. He was very well known both in the streets and unfortunately the correctional system. He was great with kids, and always wanted the best for all of us, even though he didn't follow that same advice for himself. Uncle David didn't follow the rules, and I liked that as a kid. I would soon discover that if I didn't change my mindset and my habits, I would follow his path.

2

MY YOUNGER YEARS

When our beliefs and expectations influence our behavior at the subconscious level, we are enacting what is known as a self-fulfilling prophecy. For example, if you wake up and immediately think, for no reason at all, that the day is going to be a terrible day, your attitude might make your prediction come true. You might unconsciously work to affirm your belief by ignoring the positive, emphasizing the negative, and behaving in ways that are likely to make sure you have a terrible day. Likewise, internalizing negative words directed at you can have a strong impact. Hearing and believing something that is said to you can also influence your day... not to mention your life.

Looking back on it now, when I was younger, I was scared to try anything new. I wouldn't go out of my comfort zone. I also felt I had to do more than your average bear just to get by. If I wasn't getting the positive attention I wanted, I made sure I got some sort of attention, even if it was negative.

I always felt I couldn't measure up to my older siblings and cousins. Because of my high energy I had a hard time focusing on one thing, including schoolwork, and I was just not doing my best. I didn't feel I was as athletic as my siblings, either. My brother Johnny played baseball and football and my sister Stephanie played volleyball and softball. I played one year of little league baseball. My mom was the coach. She didn't know much about baseball but to support me she agreed to coach the team along with a friend of hers. Our team had the only two female coaches in the entire baseball league. I even made the all-star team, but I'm guessing that was probably because my mom was the coach! That was the only year growing up I ever played baseball or any other team sport. Maybe I stopped playing because I only wanted my mom to coach me, and if she couldn't then I did not want to play anymore. What happened was this: because I only played a year of baseball, a relative and other members of my family would sometimes call me "The Quitter." Whether I realized it or not at the time, those words stuck with me and became a self-fulfilling prophecy.

For elementary school, I attended Thomas P. Ryan Elementary in East San Jose. For middle school, I attended Ocala Junior High, and that's where I began to get into trouble. I had some cousins in eighth grade who were knuckleheads and who hung out with the neighborhood gang. They would take people's lunch money all the time. They protected me and I looked up to them. No one would mess with me because they knew they would have to deal with my cousins. I wanted to dress like them in baggy pants and emulate them. My dad would crack down on me because he did not want me to get into trouble. It was a struggle for me to sit down and study, so I gravitated towards friends who were also getting into trouble. My energy level was always very high and still is, which probably explains why it was always so difficult for me to sit still and focus on my schoolwork. In seventh grade, I was not doing too well in school academically. I felt like fighting and hanging out was the thing to do. By the time eighth grade rolled around, I began to hang around some troubled kids in my neighborhood. I remember when I was a young kid, I didn't like to disappoint my mom or dad, but when I did, my dad would sometimes discipline me the old fashion way, which was by a thick leather belt and then say to me, "I didn't raise you this way." Of course, it hurt me but I didn't give it much thought, I just figured that this is just the way it is.

One day in eighth grade, there was a fight going on at school. Of course, I was involved. I kicked a boy in the stomach and broke a couple of his ribs. When I got to school the next day, the police were waiting for me. The boy I kicked was able to identify me. My dad had to come to the school to pick me up. The police took me into the back office and told me that they were going to charge me with assault. I was scared and stayed quiet. My dad spoke to the police and the principal in front of me. He told them he didn't raise me that way, that he was disappointed in me and that he didn't know why I hurt that boy. I threw myself at the mercy of the court and admitted what I did. I was suspended from school for a couple of days. Within a week or so, a probation officer showed up at my house. I had to promise I would not get in trouble for two years or I would be sent to juvenile hall or possibly the youth authority, which was basically a prison for kids under eighteen. I was put on probation for two years. If I stayed out of trouble, my juvenile record would be expunged. I also apologized to the boy who I assaulted. His father was there while I apologized, and to this day I can remember the look he had in his eyes towards me, like he wanted to kill me.

Instead of staying out of trouble for the next two years, I just made sure I never got caught! I got street cred from getting in trouble that day. As I entered high school, I cut school quite a bit. I hung out with older guys who had cars and introduced me to older girls, which I thought was super cool. I would hang out and cruise lowrider cars on what we called the "Boulevard" on the corner of Story & King road which is located on the east side of San Jose. I began drinking heavily. My friends and I would intimidate people and we were willing to fight anyone. My sister and her boyfriend, Eddie, were doing their best to keep me out of trouble. My sister didn't want me to get kicked out of school, or even worse, for my dad to find out what I was up to. She would write me notes to excuse me from class because I was ditching so much.

By the end of 9th grade at Mt. Pleasant High School, I had no fear of getting caught because I, along with my buddies, liked that we came off as the guys you didn't want to mess with. It felt good. I'll never forget the day a representative from Evergreen College came to my school and went around the classroom passing out information sheets about enrollment. I had no interest in enrolling. The representative wanted to give me a pamphlet anyway. After the representative put the pamphlet on my desk, I looked him in the eyes and slid it off the desk and onto the floor. No doubt about it, I was not thinking about my future.

I got a job at a deli in the 9th grade, near my house. My brother was working there also, and he and my dad got me the job. My dad wanted me to learn responsibility and the value of money. When I started working at the deli, my starting pay was $3.10 an hour and I worked about twenty hours per week. In the 9th grade I wanted to quit school to work for a magazine called *Low Rider*, which at the time was based in San Jose, that showcased customized lowered cars. A couple of my friends worked there, and they offered me a full-time job. However, I would have to quit school. When my dad learned about my bright idea, he said, "You're not going to quit school. If you quit school, you aren't going to live here for free. You'll have to pay rent!" I didn't like the sound of that, so I decided to stick it out at school.

I ended up working at the deli for three years, and even

though I wasn't internally in a good place, having a job for that long taught me how to be responsible, just as my dad had hoped. None of us learn everything we need to learn overnight. One lesson after another over time is how we gain knowledge, experience, and growth. This includes not only learning from the good times, but also from the more difficult and challenging times in our lives. We can learn lessons from everybody and every experience, even if we learn what not to do or who not to be like. My job at the deli was on the meat side. The customers would pick out the kind of meat they wanted, and I would then weigh it, package it, and price it so they could take it to the register to pay for it. The job provided money to put gas in my dad's truck so that I could get around town.

3

MY HIGH SCHOOL YEARS

In his book, *The Noticer*, Andy Andrews says: "A successful life has a great deal to do with perspective." This was so true in my life growing up. The negative things that I had heard about cops, whether they were true or not, shaped my view on all law enforcement. Because of these views, I couldn't even think of ever working in that type of career.

Back then, I was not in a good place and did not want to get caught, pulled over, or held accountable for my negative behaviors. I had family who had been in prison, and at a very young age I heard them talk about their negative law enforcement interactions. The thought of this didn't sit well with me, and it just fueled my distrust for cops. Every once in a while, there may be times when cops break the public's trust by violating their oath, but I now know that most law enforcement personnel work very hard at their jobs with integrity and professionalism. If they don't, they should be held accountable.

My neighborhood was predominantly Mexican Ameri-

-can, and many of us had the same outlook towards law enforcement. Some of the guys in the neighborhood had money, girls, and cars but weren't necessarily doing the right thing. The reality was, because I felt it was too difficult to do the right thing, I gravitated towards people who sometimes did the wrong things. It felt good to feel a sense of acceptance, even if it wasn't in a positive manner.

In high school, each neighborhood had its own "gang territory," meaning if you were there and you weren't from their neighborhood, you could get beat up. One night, we were at a house party and heard there was going to be a fight at the 7-11. We received the message that some friends of ours were going to need backup because they were outnumbered in the fight. We all went up to the 7-11 and our rivals were there. They suddenly didn't want to fight. We had a problem with that, so we started the fight. It got ugly. Our rivals ran off. Sure enough, the cops came, and we ran off. My brother, who always knew I was up to no good, heard me sneak into the room we shared at home at two o'clock in the morning. Johnny asked me, "Were you up at 7-11 tonight?" I was shocked that he would know that. So, I asked him why he thought I was up there. He said, "Because the police pulled me and my girlfriend over and told us that there was a gang fight that involved lowriders and so they thought I was a part of the fight." My brother had a beautiful lowrider with hydraulics, which was a midnight blue 1977 Ford Thunderbird. On the trunk was a gorgeous mural of the San Francisco skyline and the Golden Gate bridge at night. I had no choice but to tell Johnny, "Don't tell dad, but yeah, I was there."

One day when I was in the 9th grade, some friends of mine came and told me that my brother had gotten into a fight. Now, it must be said that my brother is much bigger and stronger than I, and could have hurt the guy really badly. However, unlike me, my brother cared about school and did not want to get suspended. He was always such a level-headed and mature guy, even as a young person. He actually thought and cared about his future.

The thought of someone fighting with one of my family members didn't sit well with me, so about fifteen of my friends and I went after the guy. A fight broke out. Let's just say, it didn't go so well for that guy. I got suspended for my involvement in the fight.

On another occasion, I was involved in another fight after school with some trouble makers that didn't even go to our school. Although we were outnumbered by the other guys, it didn't go so well for them that day. There were so many of them and it got so bad that one of the guys I knew went home, got a 30/30 rifle, and fired a couple of shots into the air to disperse the crowd.

I sure looked like a lost cause in high school. However, I had a counselor named Mrs. Sweat who was nice to me. She sat me down a couple of times when I ended up in her office. She said she was disappointed in me, and she thought I could do better. I sure remember Mrs. Sweat because she seemed like she believed in me more than I did. Unfortunately, I didn't see what she saw in me at the time. I also had a 10th grade math teacher who bought meat at the deli I worked at. He said all I had to do was show up to class and I would get a good grade. In return, I would give him a discount on his purchases at the deli. I ended up getting a B in the class.

There was a girl that I had a crush on from 9th grade to 11th grade, but I never had the chance to talk to her because she had a boyfriend who was always around her. Finally, on my first day of class in the 11th grade, there she was, sitting in my class. I purposefully sat right behind her so that I could talk to her. As I began to speak to her, she made me think that her family owned a gas station. She said she could get me a discount on gas later that evening. So, I met up with her that night so that she could take me to the gas station. As we drove up she took out a key to unlock the gas pumps, so that I could fill up my gas tank. I later found out her family didn't own that gas station, or any other one for that matter. This girl, who later became my girlfriend, was robbing the gas station and I unknowingly became her accomplice. Although she looked very sweet and innocent, she was a firecracker. I later found out that she had been sexually and physically abused as a child and she was more broken than I was. I guess we were made for each other at that time. She later told me she liked how edgy and unafraid I was.

Philosopher and entrepreneur Matshona Dhliwayo said, "You are a gift to the universe, but a package is only valuable if it allows itself to be unwrapped." Purpose and belief in that purpose is everything in life, and what I needed to learn when I was a young man is that I could achieve anything if I had a strong enough purpose.

One of the things that shook me up in the 12th grade happened during a day I cut school. My friends and I climbed into a car and drove up a hill close to a park near my house. Coincidentally, the day before I had driven there in my truck with my girlfriend, and we almost slid off the road where there was about a 150-foot cliff, which would have been disastrous. It took a tow truck to tow me back onto the road because the rear wheels of my truck were hanging over the cliff. I wanted to show my friends where this had occurred. My friend who was driving the car had been drinking, and on the way up the hill the car ran out of gas. We turned the car around and drove down the hill with the car on neutral and the engine off. We soon discovered the brakes and steering didn't work well with the engine turned off. My friend tried to avoid hitting a tree, but we ended up crashing right into it. All four of us in the car got pretty hurt that day. I got extremely cut up from the window, which shattered on me. I also ended up breaking a bone in my neck, and for a time, I had to wear a neck brace. It's a miracle I wasn't paralyzed, let alone killed, in that accident.

I just was not learning from my mistakes. The mistakes I was making were mounting up on me. I then found out that there was no way I was going to graduate because of the very few high school credits I had. What was even worse than not graduating was that I really didn't care if I did or not. Obviously, this mindset is not a good recipe for a positive future. I ended up quitting school when I found out that I wasn't graduating. After quitting school, I immediately signed up to take the General Educational Development (G.E.D.) exam. The G.E.D. is considered to be a high school equivalency certificate. The week after I had quit school, I took and passed my G.E.D. exam, quit my job at the deli, and started working full-time for a machine shop. I was about eighteen years old at this time. It was a dirty job, but I enjoyed it. Although I was never scared to work, I started to feel lost, and defeated with no sense of purpose. I was working 40 hours a week at the machine shop after dropping out of high school. My life was a day-to-day existence with no thought of the future or my past actions.

4

HIGHER PURPOSE

When I was around eleven or twelve, my dad was in a similar rut. He felt his life was not going in the right direction. My aunt and uncle invited my dad to go to church. They had invited him several times before, but he always refused to go. My dad actually made fun of my aunt and uncle for being Christians. The fact was, while my dad was a good person, he had not been making good choices for himself and our family. Finally, there was an event at church that my father agreed to attend. Once he was there, he had an overwhelming feeling to ask for forgiveness and repent. He felt that he needed God to lead him on the right path. That day, my dad and mom gave their hearts to the Lord and became Christians and they never looked back for the rest of their lives. My dad became an avid reader of the Bible. He still rode his motorcycle, but he wouldn't hang out with the same people and stopped having rowdy parties at our house. He required all of us to go to church once a week. He'd preach to everyone and would ask my friends to attend church with us. My dad's thoughts and opinions mattered to our whole family. Most of where my family is today is because my father had a big influence on them. He brought several of my family members to God and helped others find their paths without pushing or pressuring them, but would just share the word of God and let them know that God is always there for all. My dad was admired and respected, so most of the family just listened and were inspired by my father.

At eighteen years old, even though I had led a fast and troubled life, I began to have a sense I wasn't being the best person I could be. On Easter of 1984, I was at church with my family. The pastor said, "If you want to accept Jesus in your heart, ask God to forgive you and to come into your life and your heart." I did this and asked for forgiveness. To my surprise, I started crying. It was a heavy duty feeling of emotion. From that point on, I was a straight shooter, kind of like my dad. I gave my heart to God and started reading the Bible. I stopped doing knucklehead things with my old friends. That's not to say my friends disliked what I was doing. To the contrary, my friends knew my dad and I were born-again Christians and they were cool with it. When I became a Christian, several of my friends began to follow that same path with me.

Not long after my religious experience, I was watching a program on TBN (Trinity Broadcast Network), a religious channel. I saw an ad that announced the opening of a bible college in Baton Rouge, Louisiana. The school was going to be run by the famous evangelist, Jimmy Swaggart. I liked Swaggart's fiery preaching, and I just knew I had to attend that college.

I asked my dad what he thought about me going to bible college. He said, "You apply, and we'll take it from there." I could tell my dad was excited that he could have a son who would be a preacher. I called the bible college to get the application materials. I soon realized that applying was going to be tough because I only had a G.E.D., and with my horrible academic and behavioral record, there was no way I could get teacher recommendations. I figured I had nothing to lose by trying, so I mailed in my high school transcripts with my application and prayed for the best. After I applied, I didn't hear anything back from the school and since classes began in August, I figured it was in God's hands.

I finally got a call in June or July from the Dean of Admissions, Dr. Reuben J. Sequeira. I could tell right away that Dr. Sequeira was a serious guy. He said to me, "Adam Duran, this is Dr. Reuben Sequeira, the Dean of Admissions for Jimmy Swaggart Bible College." I nervously said hello. Dr. Sequeira then said, "I just have to know one thing. I'm looking at your transcripts right now. I just want to know: is it a different ballgame now for you?" I said, "Yes, sir, I gave my heart to God and I'm a different person now." There was silence on the other line. It was probably only a few seconds, but it seemed like forever to me. Dr. Sequeira then said, "Okay, we'll see you in August." I couldn't believe my ears. I thanked Dr. Sequeira and told him I wouldn't disappoint him.

I hung up the phone. I was on my way to bible college in Baton Rouge! Now, I began to feel I had a purpose. I was no longer living day-to-day. I just needed faith that I could handle the challenges that lay ahead.

5

COLLEGE YEARS

Where you want to go in life is largely dependent on the associations that can help you get there. Good associations can be found in new and fertile environments. To improve my chances of success, one of the best things I found I could do was hang out with people I admired and looked up to. My grandma, who was so very wise, used to say, "Don't tell me who you are—just tell me who your friends are and I'll tell you who you are." Quite simply, just find a way to be around people who you want to be like. Sometimes it's uncomfortable to be around people who are at a different level than you are. You may think they are above your capabilities, but believe me, they did not get there overnight. You don't have to reinvent the wheel. Follow what others are doing, who are excelling in the area you want to excel in, and in time you will excel also.

When I went off to college, my environment and associations changed, and my life changed. I left for Baton Rouge in late August of 1984. It was a brand-new start, and

I was so excited to study the Bible. I couldn't wait to get there. I had never been away from home before. Everyone was crying before I left, but my parents were very proud of me for going. I flew out of San Francisco on Delta airlines. During the plane ride, I couldn't help but think that only two years ago, I had never given college any thought and I had swiped the college information off my desk. Now the knuckleheaded kid who had been in trouble with the law was going to Bible college and wanted to be a preacher.

I arrived in Baton Rouge, disembarked the plane, and entered a very small airport. When I got outside, the humidity hit me like a ton of bricks. I felt like I couldn't breathe. I hailed a taxi to take me to the campus. The college was in a rural area, spread over several acres. This was a large organization with several buildings, a church, and two twelve-story dorm buildings for the student body. Each building was divided up for men and women. I checked in and was assigned a room and a roommate. There were only about 500 students in the entire school because it was a new college. My roommate was a guy from Texas named Robbie. He was heavy-set and played the bass guitar. In fact, that's exactly what he was doing when I walked into the dorm room and met him for the first time.

The biggest shock was when I walked into the classroom. The four-year curriculum required everyone to have a minor in the Bible, and then you could choose any major that was offered. I decided to major in evangelism. I knew it was going to be tough for me academically, but I was up for the challenge. I had hardly read a book in high school, and I sure didn't do much schoolwork leading up to this point. When they handed me a syllabus and explained what was going to be required, my head spun. I was taking seventeen credits my first semester and had five term papers to complete. I didn't even know what a term paper was! I thought it was a book report. Even when I had to do a book report back in school, I'd read the back cover, plagiarize a little, and hope for the best. This was a whole different ball game. I had no idea what I was doing!

Luckily for me, I got help from some fellow students. They had patience with me. They knew I wasn't your average church goer. Compared to many of the kids, I was streetwise and a bit rough around the edges. I didn't like anyone coming close to me. I was trying to change my ways, but it wasn't going to happen overnight. I think I came across to my fellow students as a project for them, someone they could help. Everybody at that college was willing to help anybody else.

I was kind of homesick at first, and called home every weekend. I felt out of my element. College was scary. I didn't want to fail. My church back home knew I was going to bible college. People in my circle of influence didn't often go away to college. I didn't want to let the people back home down. Also, there were not a lot of Latinos on campus, but we gravitated towards each other. Baton Rouge had a Taco

Bell, but that was about it as far as Mexican restaurants. Still, it was very inclusive. I met one of my lifelong best friends at college. Dirk, who is caucasion, was from Illinois and went on to become a preacher and missionary. Dirk was always encouraging and non-judgmental. His belief in me was, and continues to be, unwavering.

Going to college was a calling and a whim. My new friends gave me the confidence that I could succeed, even though I had dropped out of high school. I was more than I thought I was. I watched and molded myself to become more by staying in the game and getting help from other students who knew what they were doing. Even though I usually jumped all-in anyway, I learned not to be afraid of failing. My confidence was getting stronger because of my associations. I began to develop better habits during my first year of college. I was around people who were studying hard, so now I learned how to study hard and burn the midnight oil. I learned when teachers write things on the board, I had better take the time to write them down because it just might be important information. I developed an ear and eye for what to study.

As a result of my new and helpful friends, I did well my first semester. Still, the school was very strict. No nonsense was tolerated. Every student was required to attend church every morning and twice on Sunday. This routine was implemented to make sure they didn't lose any sheep, so to speak. Many of us were just eighteen years old, but all of us for the most part were there because we felt we had a "higher purpose," a calling from God, and wanted to do the right thing. Because of the quality of people I hung out with, we all kept each other in check. Everyone had high expectations and that rubbed off on me. We all wanted to convert the world. Socially it was good, too. We'd eat beignets, drink hot chocolate, and hang out at the mall or go to the Piggly Wiggly for snacks.

When I came home for Christmas break, our house looked so small. My dad and I could really talk about things now. He only wanted to talk about the Bible, and now I could do that. Most of my college teachers were skilled speakers, teachers and preachers who held doctorate degrees in divinity. I decided when I came home again for the summer that I wanted to teach and preach. I really enjoyed preaching a message to the congregation and had a burning desire to do so. When I did come home for the summer, I worked for a glass company, and at times worked at the church, too. I'd help out with Sunday school and do speaking engagements. As long as I knew the subject matter and was prepared, I found I could talk in front of any crowd, no matter how large. I had changed, and I encouraged others to change too.

Then my life changed in a way that threw me for a loop. When I came home between my sophomore and junior year, I fell in love. Lynn was a beautiful woman. Her mother knew me from a Bible study class I was teaching at my home church called Twin Palms Assembly of God in East San Jose. After I preached one day, Lynn's mom said she loved my message, and she would love for me to meet her daughter. I was more than happy to oblige. Once I saw Lynn, I almost passed out looking at her, she was so striking. I immediately invited her to a home Bible study class that I was teaching. Even though Lynn didn't grow up in the church, she had a legitimate interest in the Bible. Lynn was smart and streetwise and like me, a bit rough around the edges. Growing up, she had a difficult childhood. Her father was an abuser of drugs. She certainly had a rougher upbringing than I did. She also had become a single mother at seventeen years old. I, on the other hand, looked like someone who was going places, so the union seemed a bit strange for those looking in from the outside. When we met, her son was four years old. Lynn's being a single mother didn't matter to me. I was all in. I wanted to spend as much time as I could with her. It was so hot and heavy I wasn't sure I wanted to go back to Bible college. We were infatuated with each other and had deep chemistry. Going back to my third year of college and leaving Lynn was tough. I called her a lot and ran up the phone bill. After my third year, we planned to get married. I was impulsive about this.

6

GETTING MARRIED

I wanted to marry Lynn before I started my fourth year of college. My parents and many church people were not thrilled about it, for sure. But I was so in love with Lynn, I had made up my mind that I wanted to be with her. People may ask why I didn't just wait to get married after finishing one more year of college. After all, I had come so far and put in so much work. Looking back on my decision now, the answer is obvious: I was impulsive and infatuated and just wanted to be with Lynn and marry her. Many of the people from my family and church were not for Lynn and I getting married, so I reasoned that it must be the devil trying to stop me from doing God's will. Consequently, all of the resistance I faced just strengthened my resolve and drove me harder towards Lynn.

We got married in July of 1987 at Twin Palms church. After the wedding, Lynn and my new stepson drove across the country, over two thousand miles to Louisiana. I intended to try to finish school, but financially I knew I couldn't swing it. By December, at the end of the first semester, we found out that Lynn was almost a month pregnant. Of course, we were thrilled about it! I knew at that point we would have to adjust for the future of our growing family. I decided not to return to school. Dr. Sequeira, the man to whom I promised that I wouldn't disappoint, had no idea what I was about to do. Years later, I reached out to Dr. Sequeira and met with him. He never judged me for my decision to drop out of college. He just wanted me to follow my calling.

After Christmas, I weighed my limited options. One thing I knew was I didn't want to go back to San Jose to live. I was no longer in school in Louisiana, so there was nothing keeping me there either. Fortunately, my good friend Dirk and his wife invited me to move up with them and help work in the church he was working at in Freeport, Illinois. The Midwest was really out of my comfort zone. The town of Freeport was known for hosting the Lincoln-Douglas debate of 1858. It was also known as "Pretzel City, USA," due to a popular local German bakery known for its pretzels in the 1850s. It seemed like as good of an alternative as any.

In January of 1988, we packed up and moved from Louisiana to Illinois. We arrived in Freeport in the dead of winter. All I remember was there was lots of snow and a lot of corn fields. We moved in and lived with my buddy Dirk and his wife Bobbie until we were able to get our own place. I got a job at a janitorial company cleaning floors. Dirk also spoke to his pastor, and found opportunities for me to help out at their church with Bible study and the youth group. Lynn worked at a daycare center called We Care Daycare, which worked out well because my stepson was able to go to the daycare with her. Freeport was a small city with a population of no more than thirty thousand people. Because it was a new city for both of us, we had to constantly adjust to the weather changes (it was COLD). Although Lynn, my stepson, and I were able to adjust well, there were other factors that came into play, mostly surrounding being able to survive financially. I had not planned on having a bigger family so soon, even though I was thankful for it, but at times I felt unsettled, personally, professionally, and financially. I beat myself up that I could have made better decisions. I did a lot of soul-searching. On the other hand, there were benefits to being in yet another different environment, with different people, and a different culture. My mind began to expand, and looking back, I think continuing to be around different people made a positive difference in my life.

My son, also named Adam, was born August 11, 1988. In October 1988, we decided to move back to San Jose. Part of the decision to move back west was due to missing our families and having their support. As always, Dirk was not judgmental, and he was supportive of my decision. My retreat to San Jose as a college dropout, with a bigger family and no immediate career prospects made me think back to when, as a kid, I didn't think long-term. I felt like I was reverting to my old bad habits. However, I knew now that

I wanted more out of life. Becoming a Christian opened my eyes to the things I *didn't* want. When I went to college, I was around lots of young people who were driven by a purpose and thought bigger than I did. I started to develop a different mindset from there. When I was around other people my age who had understood how to plan, focus, and be tenacious, I started to adopt that type of mindset as well. My associations were bigger thinkers than I was, therefore I began to become a bigger thinker.

When I returned to San Jose from Illinois, I was done with my seat-of-the-pants existence. I started to plan. I decided to spend 1989 working consistently for the year and then find a better job. Eventually, I ended up getting two jobs. From 7:00 a.m. to 3:30 p.m., I worked for a company called Radius with my cousin Irvin, who helped me land the job. I looked up to Irvin because of his strong, steady, and tenacious spirit. Radius was a company that built monitors for computers. When I got off of work at 3:30 from Radius, I would start my second job at Levitz from 5:00 p.m. until about 10:00 p.m. I worked at Levitz, which was a furniture store and known by its popular slogan and jingle, "You'll love it at Levitz."

According to the plan, after a year, I began looking for another job. I saw an advertisement for a job with the Santa Clara County Department of Corrections as a Correctional Officer. I saw how much it paid, which was more than the two jobs I was currently working. That definitely inspired me to apply for the job. At first, I had concerns about my past. I was a high school dropout, a college dropout, and wondered if my less-than-stellar juvenile record would hold me back. If you don't take the chance to go for something you want, you have no chance of getting it. Don't let the fear of failure or the unknown stop you. I knew I had grown up and was a different person than when I was a teenager, and I had nothing to lose by going for it. So I went for it. In college, I had been around graduates and professors with doctorate degrees, so I figured all of that had to have rubbed off on me a little. I think so many people are hesitant to pursue their dreams because of their fear of failure and lack of confidence. Bottom line is, you always want to give it your best shot!

*Top left, is my mom, dad.
Bottom left is my brother Johnny, sister Stephanie and myself*

My sister Steph, me and Johnny. We all used to love when dad would take us for rides on his Harley.

My one year playing baseball. My mom who was my coach is on the upper left hand corner. I am on the bottom right.

Me at eight years old. My one and only time ever playing on a team sport.

My friends and I hanging out back in the day. I'm on the bottom right. 1983

Me, in my bible college dorm room in Baton Rouge La. 1986

Many of my friends would enjoy getting together and singing in the college dorms. I'm on the top left Baton Rouge, La. 1986

Academy #24 graduation 1992. I'm in a partial shadow two guys up from the bottom on the right.

LIVE LIFE ON PURPOSE

This is the Main Jail where my career started in 1992.

Sheriff's office headquarters

LIVE LIFE ON PURPOSE

My father pinning my sergeant badge on me

LIVE LIFE ON PURPOSE

Mt. Pleasant Christian Center, formerly known as Twin Palms Church where my life changed.

Some of the books that help keep me focused on a growth mindset and my purpose.

LIVE LIFE ON PURPOSE

Tracy man meets his goal on way to Boston

By Bob Brownne
Tracy Press

This year's Boston Marathon signals Adam Duran's achievement of a lifelong goal.

"It's the Olympics for marathoners, to get there," he said, adding that serious marathon runners are always asked if they've been to the Boston Marathon.

"Everybody wants to know that. That's one of the first questions," Duran said. "My big day was qualifying. It validated me as a runner."

Duran, 48, tried four times to meet the time standard for the Boston Marathon before he qualified May 26 at the Mountains to Beach Marathon from Ojai to Ventura.

and months," Duran said. "I'd wake up at night thinking, 'I can't believe I qualified.' It meant that much to qualify."

Duran, a 12-year Tracy resident and a correctional officer for Santa Clara County, sees running as a natural endeavor. His passion for the sport matches his high-energy personality.

"Everybody grew up running. It's a natural thing for humans, to walk, then run," he said.

He explained that he learned to love running long distances during his law enforcement training, as a complement to a stressful occupation.

"It helps me decompress, totally. It's just a special gift that I've been blessed with," he said.

Now Duran looks for

2013 marathon and knew that what he was seeing would change the nature of the event.

"Every runner, every American, I feel, was a

nent place in the 118-year history of the event. He said this year's theme, "Boston Strong," is meaningful even for a first-time Boston

OBJECTIVE ATTAINED: Adam Duran qualified for the 2014 Boston Marathon after repeated attempts.
Bob Brownne / Tracy Press

I was featured in an article in the Tracy Press when I qualified for the Boston Marathon.

A picture of me at the Boston Marathon finish line

The Wellesley College scream tunnel girls at mile 13 on the Boston Marathon course.

While in the middle of writing this book I ran my first ultra marathon at the Quicksilver 50K.

LIVE LIFE ON PURPOSE

My Uncle David

LIVE LIFE ON PURPOSE

I'm thankful for having such a supportive sister, Stephanie and my brother in law Eddie.

My Uncle Nick and Aunt Mary

My good friends Dirk and his wife Bobbie who always supported me

One of the last pictures taken with my dad. Mom, Johnny, dad, me and sister Stephanie.

Adam Jr and I flew down to Phoenix to watch some championship boxing in Nov. 2021.

7

DON'T GIVE UP

Eminem famously rapped, "Success is my only option, failure is not." Venturing into a new career would teach me how to be an overcomer.

When I applied to be a Correctional Officer for Santa Clara County in 1990, I had to take some preliminary steps: there was a background check, a written exam, and a psychological exam. I had to talk to a psychiatrist, undergo a polygraph test, and take a physical. If I passed all of those steps, I would then be offered a job on the condition that I could graduate from the training academy. After completing all the prerequisites required for the job, I felt optimistic about my chances, but then was told there was a hiring freeze. I didn't see that coming. Many times, life just doesn't go the way you had planned for it to go, but the important thing is that you don't give up. When you persevere through challenges, it builds grit, and character. Due to some budget issues the county had at the time, they could not hire until those issues were resolved. The Personnel Department told me to call back in two weeks to see how things were going. Exactly two weeks later, I called back. I was told again to call back, but this time in three weeks. I kept calling back when they told me to. Whenever they would tell me to call back, I would put it on my calendar to call back exactly when they told me to do so. In fact, I called back so often that everybody in their office knew me by name. However, the time periods between callbacks kept getting longer and longer. Fortunately, I was still working two jobs, because the hiring freeze ended up lasting two years, which was longer than I ever imagined it would take.

While I waited out the hiring freeze, I started running to get in shape. The goal was to be fit enough to survive the boot camp type of exercises at the training academy. I then started to visualize not just passing the physical tests but doing so with flying colors. Failure was not an option! Visualization is a powerful tool to use in attaining your goals. When my shift at Radius ended at 3:30 p.m., I would go for a run, then shower and start my shift at 5:00 p.m. at Levitz, which was only a couple miles away from Radius. While there was no guarantee I would even be offered a job as a Correctional Officer, I did not let the thought of not getting offered the job overtake me. I stayed the course.

Instead, I thought it was a matter of when, not if, I would get the job. I wanted to succeed. My time in college helped develop that mindset in me—to succeed. When I started running, I began to push harder. Running became the outlet that helped me decompress from work and life. It was also training me in patience, which has never been one of my strong suits.

During the two-year hiring freeze, I persevered. Thankfully, Lynn was supportive about what I was doing. I was 24 when I started the application process with the department. I was not the same person I was when I was a youngster. During the two years of waiting, I kept working my two jobs to pay the bills. I was tenacious and did not give up.

After two years of calling about when the hiring freeze would be over, I finally got the call I had been waiting for. There was a message on my answering machine. When I pressed "Play," a recorded voice said, "Great news, Adam, we're hiring again! Come on in so that you can pick up an application packet." Due to the length of time which had passed I would need to update my application. I immediately called the personnel department. This was about 4:30 p.m. and I was told that the office closed at 5:00 p.m. I got off the phone, drove twenty minutes to the personnel department, and arrived at 4:50 p.m. to pick up the packet so that I could take it home and update it. That's how badly I wanted the job! I had developed grit to be tenacious and not give up on my dream and it was finally paying off.

I started my ten-week academy training in October of 1992. I found out I got into the academy about two or three months before that, but I had to go through the preliminary tests all over again, except the initial written test I had taken two years before. I had no other thoughts other than I was going to make it and I was going to do my best to graduate at the top of my class. All my running had paid off, because I ended up being the second fastest of my academy. The fastest of the class was a guy from Kenya who came to the United States on a running scholarship for San Jose State University. I graduated with a final academic grade of 92%. I had a purpose and a goal, and I achieved it. I had been visualizing doing this for two years. Failure was not an option. Eminem was right!

8

TROUBLE IN PARADISE

You've heard these sayings before. Life throws you curveballs, and you need to be able to hit them. Let your struggles make you, not break you. Some people get driven down and some people get driven up. It's a choice how we will respond to the challenges that life brings us. If you believe there is nothing that can beat you, it won't beat you. Life happens for us, not to us. If you believe that life happens to you, then you have become a victim; if you believe you are a victim, then you become powerless to course-correct. But, on the other hand, if you believe that life happens for you, that empowers you to course-correct. We can overcome any challenge if we believe we can. I'm here to say that challenges can either diminish you, define you, or develop you. When the going gets tough, and you don't give up, it will strengthen your mind and your resolve. Believe me, I know this to be true!

In December of 1992, I certainly had no reason to be anything but optimistic about my future. I hit the ground running in my new law enforcement career. I was assigned to work as a Correctional Officer at the Main Jail, which is a maximum-security jail in Santa Clara County. The Main Jail is where we kept the most violent inmates with some of the most violent crimes. All new officers underwent constant training and tests. Training officers were assigned to each newly hired officer to assure they knew how to do their job. I knew I had made the right decision, even though some inmates were intimidating and violent.

Professionally, I had achieved one goal, but I had more goals. I wanted to successfully complete training and get off the six-month probationary period which was required for each new officer. I kept focusing on one thing after another to go through the process. I was riding high and all seemed good. However, a year into my new career, trouble began brewing at home with my marriage. I had to work the day shift for half of my training, and then be reassigned to work the night shift for the rest of my training. During these night shifts, my wife started hanging out with some of her cousins who had been known to be up to no good. I didn't like the idea of her spending so much time with them, but Lynn reassured me her cousins had changed for the better. She said that because I was away working nights, she was bored at home, and wanted to hang out with them so that our kids could play with their kids. I had never had any reason in the past to doubt her, so I didn't doubt that she was being forthcoming with me this time.

Shortly after Lynn started hanging out with her cousins, I started noticing inconsistencies in her behavior, and things that did not make sense. I was having a hard time contacting Lynn. One morning, after my shift was over at 6:00am, I came home from work and noticed her 1990 Nissan Sentra wasn't there. At first, I thought she hadn't come home from her cousin's house. However, when I went inside of our house, Lynn was there in bed. I asked her where the kids were. She said they were asleep, then I asked her where the car was, because it was not in the driveway. She said that if it's not there it must have been stolen, so I called 911 to report our car had been stolen, but was informed it wasn't stolen—it had been repossessed. I had no idea how that could have happened. I asked Lynn about it and she said it had to be a mistake. The reason she had no idea the car was gone, was because it had been repossessed in the middle of the night. It turned out it was not a mistake. She hadn't made payments on the car for three months. Things just fell apart from there. I never knew Lynn to smoke, but I began finding cigarettes in my car. Lynn told me that her cousins must be leaving them accidently in the car. Now, I began to wonder what really was going on, because her explanations were just not adding up. I was constantly searching the house for clues. In the custodial setting, if things look and feel out of place you have to investigate as to why that is, and I was pretty good at it. No matter what Lynn told me, she knew I wasn't buying into it and I was asking lots of questions and doing my own research, and this rattled her. I noticed that Lynn's daily habits were changing, and from time to time she would spend the night at her cousin's house. One day I came home and was shocked that our electric company had shut off the electricity, the house phone was shut off, and my landlord informed me the rent hadn't been paid for three months. I couldn't believe it. All of this was happening because Lynn was spending so much time with her cousins, she began developing the bad habits they had. She was spending our money partying instead of paying the bills. It was an example of what happens when bad associations come into play.

Fortunately, I had good friends and family to help get me through this crisis. I still had to go to work and have someone watch my stepson and Adam. Lynn tried to work things out and said all the right things, but it was just talk. American poet Maya Angelou says, "When people show you who they are, believe them." She eventually got arrested and booked into jail for drug possession at the same jail I worked at. She got pulled over and drugs were found in the car. The car was impounded again. I was working upstairs on the fifth floor of the jail when I received a call from the booking department, which was located in the basement. They informed me that my wife had been arrested and was being booked into custody. I could not believe this was happening! I was devastated and of course embarrassed.

My family was falling apart but I knew I couldn't fall

apart because I had kids to think about. I needed to keep it together for them and to continue working to be able to provide for them, and to be able to settle all the debts that Lynn had racked up. I knew I had to go to work and get it done. I had to remain hard working and professional on my job. Any chance I got, I would try to distract myself and the kids from the pain of what we were going through by taking them to the movies and to play at local parks. My kids kept asking where their mom was and when she was coming home. Every time they would ask for their mom, it felt like a punch in my gut. There was no easy answer for that one.

Things eventually got so bad that I had to move in with my parents. My mom and mother-in-law watched the kids when I went to work. I remember thinking that all I wanted to do was sleep, because it hurt too much to be awake. It was hard to eat because I had no appetite. Food tasted bland and had no taste. Even stranger, was that colors all looked the same, and nothing stood out. Looking back, I think I was experiencing something I had never gone through before, which was some form of depression. There I was with two kids, trying to keep it all together while everything seemed to be falling apart.

Lynn served her first term in jail, then was released a few weeks later. Things never got better for her. She ended up doing at least two prison terms for multiple offenses. I sure didn't see that trouble coming. Up until this time and throughout our marriage, Lynn was a good wife and mother who was always accountable and dependable. I think part of Lynn's problems stemmed from her abusive childhood, and unresolved internal issues. Due to that, she lost focus on what really mattered in life. I've read that when women have an absent and or an abusive father, this can really cause internal emotional damage, and eventually lead them to struggle with themselves and their relationships. During this time, and prior to her prison terms I still wanted our marriage to work, so I tried to help her. I think deep down inside Lynn wanted help, but she was too far into her addiction that she felt she couldn't get out.

Eventually, I had no choice but to begin the divorce process. She was not in a good position to be able to properly care for herself or the kids. By the end of the year, the divorce was finalized. It was so difficult. She promised me she wouldn't do drugs anymore, but she continued to do so. Again, bad associations can do real damage. The Bible says in 1 Corinthians 15:33 "Don't be misled: bad company corrupts good character." I'll never forget that one night while I was working, Lynn called me up crying, saying she didn't want to come home but had nowhere to stay for the night. She asked me to help get her a room for the night in a motel, but I did not have any money at the time. So, she asked if she could spend the night in my car in the parking lot, so I reluctantly said she could. It was a cold night, so I brought her out a jail blanket so that she wouldn't get so cold in my car. When I got off duty at six in the morning, Lynn asked if I could drop her off at a nearby Denny's restaurant. Even though it was breaking me to do so, I took her. As we drove to the restaurant, I told her I would get her any kind of help that she needed, but she refused. I was confused and hurt because I just could not understand why she would not want any help. My heart sank as I drove away from Denny's, because I still loved her and could see her in my rearview mirror just standing in front of the restaurant looking cold and helpless. I wanted to turn the car around to pick her up and get her some help but I knew she would not get in my car, so I continued driving away.

Despite the overwhelming problems I had at home, I knew I had to keep showing up to work and stay professional, which was very difficult for me during this time, to say the least. I just kept my focus at work no matter what. I stayed in the game and didn't quit. I didn't ask my parents for any financial help because they were letting me live with them rent-free. I borrowed $1,300 from a friend to get the car out of impound and I paid him back over four months.

1993 to 1994 was indeed rough for me. I felt broken, but with the help of my faith, family, and friends I was confident I would somehow get through this time in my life. No matter what was happening, I would hang on to the scripture in Philippians 4:13 "I can do all things through Christ which strengthens me." I was young, trying to get through life, but I still had an instinct not to quit. This life wasn't just about me, but about us. I had kids to support, a life to live, and a family who loved me, so I knew that even though things looked and felt terrible, I would get through this. I kept going to church and leaned on my faith. I stayed social with the good people in my life. I used the pain as fuel to get through and to propel me to better days ahead. Too many people give up too early before they become successful. Life can beat you up. It's full of challenges that can distract you from your purpose. Quitting when the going gets tough can deprive you of long-term success. I'm glad I learned that lesson or I would've missed out on what lay ahead for me. In reality, life will always challenge you, and this is how we grow. We don't grow when things are easy for us, we grow when we are challenged. Through resistance in life is how we grow. If you are a weight lifter and want to get stronger, you will need to add more weight, so that you could have some resistance and eventually get stronger.

9
CONTROL YOUR ATTITUDE

Motivational speaker Brian Tracy said, "You cannot control what happens to you, but you can control your attitude toward what happens to you, and in that, you will be mastering change rather than allowing it to master you." I couldn't agree with that more. If you can't change or control a situation, the best thing you can do is control your thoughts, and not let your thoughts control you. If you control your thoughts, you will change how you view the situation (Perspective) and subsequently turn the negative into a positive. The old adage "Is the glass half full or half empty?" is very applicable. You are looking at the same glass and yes, it is half full but also half empty. How you view the glass will either be a positive or a negative, and this can either fuel you or defeat you. In my nearly 30-year career in law enforcement, this was confirmed for me many times over.

I did my best to stay away from office politics. I felt it didn't serve me to get into that in such a large bureaucracy. I learned quickly that if I couldn't change a situation I would learn to accept it. I would not let it affect my attitude or work habits. I refused to let anything control me or what I do. I worked for the Sheriff's Department and I was going to do my best to be the best that I could be. I did my job and had a good work ethic. I noticed that when people got involved with office politics, they tended to get a bit sour toward the department and they did not seem to be the most fulfilled officers. Many people are always looking for what is wrong instead of what is right. If you are always looking for what is wrong, you will find it, but if you're always looking for what is right, you will find that also. I try to be mindful, to be able to accept things that are out of my control. If the sun is setting tonight, I'm not going to fight it. If the sun is rising, I won't fight it. People who try to change things they can't control don't end up in a good place emotionally or mentally. Fighting the system doesn't work in every instance. I'm not saying we shouldn't try and fix things that should be fixed, but what I am saying is that where your focus goes your energy will flow. Therefore, be mindful of what you focus on. In politics, people often fight things they don't fully understand, and they sometimes assume everything and everyone is against them. First of all, that is just not the truth, and second of all, it just takes too much energy from you when you could use your energy for thinking and doing something more positive and productive. At work there were times when I didn't necessarily like a new policy and or procedure, but if I am not going to voice it or write it up to try and effect change, then it would do me no good to stew about it. As a result of this mindset, I chose to have a positive attitude and be careful that it didn't take any positive energy from me. Over time, I began to develop an ability to accept things and be okay with the things I couldn't change. Like the Serenity Prayer says, "God grant me the Serenity to accept the things I cannot change, the Courage to change the things I can, and the Wisdom to know the difference." My mindset is that if I had no choice but to be placed in the middle of the Mojave desert and there were no other alternatives, I will find a way to accept it, live there in the sand and heat and be happy there. That's how I think. I make the best of it no matter what. When life throws you lemons, make lemonade out of it. I'm just determined to make the best of every situation. Abraham Lincoln said, "People are as happy as they make up their minds to be." I found out that happiness really is a choice that we make every day. It's not what happens to us, it's how we choose to respond to what happens to us that will make the difference in how our life will go.

Now there have been times where I took positions, but I didn't know if I'd like them. Being a leader, being in middle management, you must own it and sell it to those reporting to you even if you don't agree with it. Those times can be challenging for sure. It may not be the most popular directive, but you have to sell it. Which raises the question: how do you "sell it?" What I have learned is you must be honest, otherwise your staff will see right through you. Also, what I've found to be important is that staff want to be heard. Listen to their concerns so that you can have a better understanding of their apprehension at accepting something new. You want them to have a vested interest. They want to be heard and they should be. You need to care about their perspective, because it's valuable not only to them but to the organization. I have found that your team will go with it if they feel they have been heard out as opposed to shoving it down their throats. A great example of this principle in action was when a new timekeeping system was implemented. I wasn't a fan of it, but I couldn't change it, so I informed the troops that it's a departmental policy that was meant to make it easier for the payroll keepers and would help keep us all honest, including me.

In my job as a lieutenant, I would often take daily walks around the facility, which was made up of many buildings. I would walk the facility and meet with the deputies face-to-face. I felt like that made a difference. I would show my presence and I would do my best to get to know each of them personally. That's how I consistently conducted myself. The sergeants would also have BBQs and recognize milestone events, such as birthdays, to help with team morale and keep our officers engaged. Recognizing that we all worked in a dangerous and stressful environment, I wanted to always be motivating and optimistic for the entire team.

The way I stayed positive and optimistic was by having a daily routine. I woke up two hours before my work shift began. Waking up early allowed me time to prepare my mind and body for what the day might bring. I would read for at least half an hour, run at least five miles, then come back home to take a cold shower. Then, I would go to work to begin my shift. This routine enabled me to maintain a positive mental attitude throughout the day.

Every four or five years I would apply to work in different units within the department. I wanted to expand my expertise in the workplace. If there was an opening in a unit that I wanted to work at, I would apply to work there. I always wanted to challenge myself. I strived to have a growth mindset. Our effort is the one thing we all have control over. Otherwise, there is a tendency for our minds to get complacent and subsequently accept whatever comes our way. That type of complacency is not a recipe for success.

Despite my plans and making sure I was well-rounded in my career, I didn't think about promoting to a sergeant for about twenty years. The rank structure for the Sheriff's department is a paramilitary type of structure: deputy correctional officer, sergeant, lieutenant, captain, and assistant sheriff. Why did I wait so long? Looking back on it, perhaps I had a bit of fear of the unknown, but I also realized I had never let that stop me before. I now understand I needed to step out of my comfort zone. At that time, the openings didn't happen very often. Then there was an air of "If I don't take the test now, who knows how long it will be before it will be offered again?" I took the county administered test sometime around 2012 for the sergeant position. Anywhere between 150 and 300 people were vying for the few sergeant positions that were available at that time. The very first time I tested, I didn't pass. It turned out that I had some brushing up to do. I did not let that get me down. I vowed that I would never fail another county test again. I studied for two years to get prepared for when the test came up again, and I would be prepared to pass it. I was being taught math strategies by three different instructors. You really didn't need math to be a sergeant, but they wanted to know you possessed problem solving skills. I thought, "They may not pick me to be sergeant but I'm going to make it difficult for them not to pick me." I ended up passing the test the next time the test was offered in 2014.

When I first got promoted to sergeant it was a trying time in the sheriff's department. There was a tragedy that took place in the jail. Three deputies were accused of a horrible crime. This took place in the jail I worked at, and the deputies were part of my team. Many of the deputies on the team could not believe these three deputies were capable of their involvement with this tragedy. I always did my best to reassure the deputies on our team to "Let the process ride out." I explained to my team that the deputies who were charged will have their day in court. The truth will come out, and we could not allow this event to distract us from doing our jobs. I, along with my fellow sergeants, did our best to help keep morale up. During this time, our job was very stressful for all of us. I would tell the deputies to stay healthy in body and mind and to have patience. I would constantly encourage them to stay positive and do positive things in their lives to help them decompress, like exercise, spending time with their families, and eating right. I tried to diffuse the distrust and frustration that some felt towards the department at one of the most difficult times in the department's founding since 1850. Even though I was a newly promoted sergeant, I wanted to give them hope and encouragement that tomorrow will be a brighter day. During tough and challenging times in our lives, we all could use some encouragement.

I applied the same lessons I had learned in 2014 when I was looking to be promoted again, this time to the rank of lieutenant in 2019. To prepare for the next rung on the ladder, I began studying for the promotional exam for the rank of lieutenant. A total of eleven sergeants tested for the promotion, and out of eleven, there were only two promotions. Once again, I didn't get selected. As usual, I didn't like the feeling of not succeeding. Unlike when I initially didn't pass the sergeants test, this time made me second-guess my future with the department. I even thought about retiring, but a friend of mine believed in me, and told me if I really wanted it, I would need to stop wavering and to focus on the promotion. During the first test, my friend knew that I hadn't given it my best effort and reminded me that that was out of character for me. So, following the first test she told me that if this was something I truly wanted, I would need to be all-in. Right then, I decided to commit and focus and achieve my goal of becoming a lieutenant if and when it came up again. One of the ways I used to help me focus is to have faith and visualize what I wanted. I would internally see myself as what I wanted to become, before I became it. Before I became a sergeant, I first saw myself as a sergeant. However, it does take action, not merely faith and visualization to get wherever you want to go. The Bible (NIV) says in James 2:17 "Faith by itself, if it is not accompanied by action, is dead." You have to prepare yourself by studying or doing what it takes to be able to achieve whatever goal you are after. It's also very important to surround yourself with people who support and encourage you, but also who are honest with you.

Even though there were no other lieutenant positions available, and it could be years before another one came up, I took my friend's advice to go all-in and to commit to study even if no promotional opportunities came up. At the time, I was living in a different city, so to help prepare myself for the promotion that wasn't available, I sold my house to move closer to my job, just in case the opportunity for promotion would come up. It takes action! I was all-in! Then, a few months later, out of nowhere, a lieutenant position opportunity came up again. No one in the department saw that one coming. By this time, I had been studying for almost a year. This time I knew I was better prepared to take the test. After my oral board interview, I exited the interview room and pumped my fist in the air because I knew I had done my best. As I drove away from where the test was held, I saw a deputy I knew. I pulled over to say hello to him and he asked me what I was doing at headquarters. I told him I had just taken the lieutenant's test. He asked me how I did, and I said, "I nailed it." I told him that they may not pick me but I was going to make it very difficult for them not to pick me. I had studied for almost a year, sold my house, had faith and visualized this scenario happening. Once again, like my previous promotion, I received a call from the Sheriff and her executive staff informing me they were promoting me to lieutenant. I was beyond thankful and appreciative that I was able to attain another goal of mine.

I was ready to work any shift or any amount of hours that this next promotion required. My faith, running, and my reading helped me to decompress when I needed to. It made me feel present in the now. Motivational speaker Jim Rohn said it best: "Either you run the day, or the day runs you." And speaking of running…

10

CHALLENGING YOURSELF

The science is in: exercise can help you have a more positive mindset and can help to alleviate stress. Physical well-being is a factor in overall well-being. If you don't feel your best, how can you ever expect to be your best? When I started running in 1990, it was strictly to train for the academy. I was more of a recreational runner, six miles here and six miles there. I ran some 10ks, but nothing really competitive. By 1997, I had met people who were better runners than I was. It's all in associations, right? I picked the brains of people who ran marathons and I got to thinking that maybe I could run a marathon, too. I don't think I had even run a half-marathon at that time, but that didn't matter to me. I went all-in and signed up for a marathon. I talked to a couple of guys I knew who had run one marathon each, and told them I was a little worried because I had never run a marathon before. I asked for their advice on how I should approach this new challenge. I admitted that despite my great ambition to run a marathon,

I didn't know if I could actually be successful. One of the guys said, "We ran all the time in the Marines. When we got tired, the trick was finding something you can mentally use to motivate you." He went on to say, "If someone had a gun to your mom's head and said, 'Run 26.2 miles,' I have a feeling you would find a way to run 26.2 miles." Well, that made sense and confirmed to me that a strong mindset is what it would take to get it done.

I'll never forget that during my first marathon, after twenty miles, every single step hurt. The pain vibrated through my entire body, but I kept at it, even though thoughts of quitting ran through my mind several times. I just couldn't get myself to go through with quitting. I actually made it across the finish line with a time of around 3 hours and 40 minutes. My recovery was slow and painful. I couldn't walk without pain for a week. I didn't really have a strategy to run the marathon, I just knew I wanted to run it and not fail. There is an old saying which says, "If you fail to plan, you are planning to fail." Well, I didn't fail but I came mighty close to it, that's for sure. Another reason I couldn't quit was because lots of my buddies at work knew I would be running the marathon and the thought of returning to work failing at my run was too great a cost for me. I couldn't let them down, but even more than that, I couldn't let myself down. However, after the pain I endured, I vowed that I would never again run a marathon.

A few years after running that first marathon, I began

to become a better runner. I kept reflecting on how the marathon had beat me up, and I didn't like those thoughts. So, I decided I needed to take revenge on that marathon, and this time beat it up. I ran another one, and I had a better plan and better training than I did for the first one. There was pain, but a lot less of it. I also had a better recovery. Encouraged by my progress, I thought maybe one day I could qualify for the famous Boston Marathon. Among my friends, I didn't know anyone who was running like I was. I was running blind, so to speak, so I started reading books on how to train for marathons. I upped my training and mileage. I got better the more I learned.

The Boston Marathon is traditionally held on Patriot's Day, the third Monday of April. The event began in 1897 and was inspired by the success of the first marathon competition in the 1896 Summer Olympics. It is the world's oldest annual marathon and ranks as one of the world's best-known long-distance road racing events. Its course runs from Hopkinton in southern Middlesex County to Copley Square in Boston. To qualify, you have to run a Boston Athletic Association-sanctioned marathon course within the previous eighteen months from the date of the Boston marathon. I first tried to qualify in December of 2008 for the April 2010 Boston Marathon. I ran the CIM (California international Marathon) in Sacramento to qualify, which was a Boston-certified course. I hit the course and was feeling pretty good. I was on point until mile 22, and then I fell apart. I had shocking cramps. I felt like my legs were stiff and freezing up on me. My knees refused to bend. It was like I was running on stilts. The cramps soon radiated all over my body. While I didn't let the pain stop me, it did slow me down. I kept thinking I could make the qualifying time of three hours and 25 minutes. As I ran through the pain and towards the finish line, I thought, I might still be able to make it, but I couldn't get my legs to run any faster and I began to slow down and my hopes of qualifying slipped away. I missed it by a matter of minutes. The thought of not qualifying when I had worked so hard was heartbreaking. I vowed to come back and qualify another time.

In 2010, I decided to try to qualify again. I met up with a running group called the Running Addicts. They offered to help me train. My next qualifying marathon was in March 2011 at the Modesto marathon. I was following different programs and techniques to get it done this time. I had pacers who helped me. But, I fell apart again, this time at mile 23. My whole body felt like it was shutting down on me as I crossed the finish line. Now what? Twice I had not made the qualifying time for Boston. But I knew I could do it.

I let myself recover then found another marathon to run. In August 2011, I ran the Santa Rosa marathon and you guessed it, I again fell apart at mile 23. After my recovery, I vowed to continue to fight to qualify. This time I chose to run the Mountain to Beach Marathon, in May 2012. The good news was I made it past mile 23 without falling apart, but the bad news was that I fell apart at mile 24. The several letdowns began to take its toll on me. No matter how positive of a mindset I had kept, the thought began to occur to me that maybe I wasn't cut out to run the qualifying time for the most prestigious marathon in the world. It took me a while to recover from the constant disappointment of not qualifying for Boston, but I was determined to do whatever I had to do to qualify. My attitude was, "I am either going to qualify for Boston or I'll die trying."

I was bombarded with different ideas about programs and techniques to make a qualifying time for Boston. My running group kept encouraging me. It was my son Adam who unknowingly helped me with my breakthrough. He had given me a gift card to Barnes & Noble bookstore. After some browsing, I bought a book called, *The Hansen Marathon Method*. That book had some new tricks for my training that I implemented. My fifth attempt at qualifying for Boston, I ran the Mountain to Beach Marathon again, but this time I used the new Hansen Marathon Method, and I remember thinking I was going to qualify or die trying. At mile 23 I felt good, but I was scared I'd fall apart again. The 3 hour 25 minute pacer who I was running with said that if I felt good at 24 miles, then I should pick up my pace and run ahead of him. I waited until mile 25. This time I felt different and I hadn't frozen up yet. At mile 25, the pacer again encouraged me to run ahead of him, and at that moment I decided this was the day I was going to qualify for Boston.

I started to increase my pace and once the finish line was in sight, I ran even faster and finished the race with a strong finishing kick in 3 hours 23 minutes and 22 seconds. When I crossed the finish line I realized I had just qualified for the historic Boston Marathon after years of trying with multiple attempts, and I couldn't help but to become a bit emotional. I finally qualified for Boston that day! The fact that I had barely made the cut off with only 8 seconds to spare didn't matter to me. Losing sleep, bleeding, getting beat up, the multiple rough recoveries—it was all worth it.

I ran the Boston Marathon for the first time in April of 2014. I wanted to appreciate the moment and take it all in, especially since it was the year after the horrible terrorist attack that had taken place the prior year. The year I ran it, it seemed that the whole city was out on the course supporting the runners. Before and after the marathon, almost everywhere throughout the city, if you wore the official Boston Marathon jacket, you were treated like royalty (#Bostonstrong). I did not have to wait in any lines and was shown a lot of respect, as were all the runners. As I ran the 26.2-mile course from Hopkinson, through the historic towns and into Boston, it was everything I thought it would be and then some. I truly enjoyed looking around at the historic landmarks. The halfway point at Mile 13 was a big deal. It was located at Wellesley college, which is a private women's college, and is known as "The Scream Tunnel." The women students lined up along Central Street and offered their loud support for the runners. They also offered kisses to the runners as a motivation for us. And, motivate us they did! It seemed like there were hundreds of female students hanging over the guard rails screaming at us to kiss them.

Since 2014, I qualified for Boston three more times in a row and ran it twice. Being in a small and select group of runners who qualify for Boston from 110 countries is a great honor. On weekends for my long run, my buddy Juan and I run up to a half marathon almost every week. Training for marathons reinforced my belief that once you achieve your goal it gives you the confidence that you are limitless. Take Roger Bannister, being the first one to run the four-minute mile, for example. Once Bannister broke that barrier (people said it was impossible to break it), in the next few years, several other people ran sub-four-minute miles! Why? Because they knew it was now possible. So be a trailblazer. You have to believe in yourself, and you can't quit what you're doing. You don't know how close you are to succeeding. When people quit on a goal they are after, they'll never know if they could have succeeded if they kept trying. If the square peg is not going into the circle hole, try a different peg. But do not quit. Try different strategies. If you believe in yourself nothing can stop you! While writing this book, I became an Ultra Marathon Runner by running a 50k/31 mile trail run which included 6,000 feet of climbing, and although I vowed never to run an Ultra Marathon, my 99two friends encouraged me to join them on this run. I didn't know totally what I was getting into, but wasn't scared to give it a try. My mindset I developed is to go all-in and never fail. During this long run, my mind became tired and weakened and I wanted to find a way out of it. When my buddy saw the discouraged look in my eyes he encouraged me not to quit, because he knew that I was capable of finishing the run. I ended up completing my first ever ultra-marathon. Remember, it is all about associations. Be around people who want to see you succeed! They will catapult your life to a different level.

11

ASSOCIATIONS ON PURPOSE AND OTHER GOOD HABITS

There are many other practical things people can do today to positively change their life. For starters, be around people who are positive! If I'm around people who tend to be negative and not positive, I remove myself from them. There is a quote from author Jon Gordon that says, "Being positive doesn't mean you ignore reality. It means you maintain hope, optimism, and faith in order to create a better reality." The times I was alone in my life, I would surround myself with books and YouTube videos about people who were positive and successful. I wanted to surround myself with good people, so I removed the negativity to maintain a certain optimistic mindset. Time is valuable, you can't get it back, so you have to choose carefully who you choose to spend your time with. I met plenty of good people but found that they weren't good for me. In those cases, I had to disassociate from them. I want to believe in people but there are times when people are not who they say they are, so in those times I had to limit those associations. I try to live congruently with who I believe I am. It's confusing for me to deal with people who won't do what they say. Once again, the quote by Maya Angelou: "When people Show you who they are, believe them."

I want to add value to help others avoid the pitfalls that I went through in my life, and show them a positive way to live and how they can thrive by using some of the tips and techniques that have worked for me and I know can work for them also. Billionaire investor Ray Dalio advocates doing a stress test not only in the financial world, but also in your own personal associations and friendships. Make a habit of being around those who have a history of doing well. Those are the people you should try to be around. Do a stress test of the people in your life. Are their actions congruent to who they say they are? Don't feel bad about outgrowing people who had the chance to grow with you.

In an age where social media, news, and music program--ming can be negative and depressing, there are plenty of things you can do to stay positive. Most importantly, don't let your thoughts race unchecked. An unchecked mind will generally gravitate towards the negative, and that will affect your emotions and mood. It's our job to make ourselves happy; IT'S A CHOICE! Therefore, it's through our thoughts that we become happy or not. If your mind is constantly racing toward negative thoughts, what should you do? A few things that will help are exercising, eating healthier, and thinking about the things you have instead of the things you don't. Also, hang out with people who are positive and optimistic and generally happy. You will begin to adopt more of a happy demeanor.

Just wanting to be positive and live a positive life is not enough. Motivation is fleeting but good habits are long lasting. For example, I run, I fill my mind with books, I write in a journal, I meditate, and I pray. When a negative thought comes your way, replace it with a positive one. It's going to get dark tonight, but it will be light in the morning. There are two mountain tops for every valley. There is no downside to having good habits, or habit stacking. Exercise will help you become more optimistic along with eating healthier food. I have gotten something positive from every book I've read. Happiness is the pursuit and realization of a worthy goal. It's not money or fame! I have to live with me my whole life, so why not stack healthy habits so I can thrive? I can't give my best if I'm not feeling my best. The mind is a muscle. The more you use it the stronger it gets. You should challenge your mind. You don't have to take cold showers or run marathons, but you should do a little something every day that moves you closer to being the best version of yourself. Get out of your comfort zone; if not, you will not be able to live up to your potential.

Habit stacking has a compound effect. For example, I will go running tomorrow because it's good for me. I had better drink more water today because I'm going to run tomorrow. I'm going to eat well because I'm going to run tomorrow. I'm going to get enough sleep because I'm going to run tomorrow. Habit stacking is the process of doing little positive things, one after another, and in time, they pay off. If you eat poorly today, you won't die tomorrow. If you eat healthy today, you won't suddenly be healthy tomorrow. But over time, habitually doing either one will result in a positive or negative outcome.

Nothing comes easy. People want immediate gratification, and don't understand that it takes time to see the benefits of implementing good habits. If someone ate a bad high-calorie unhealthy meal today and gained 100 pounds tomorrow, they would never eat that type of meal again. But, if they eat a high-calorie unhealthy meal every day, over time they will probably gain quite a bit of weight and maybe suffer health issues as well. Nothing happens overnight, so they are not totally aware of the long-term consequences of their daily habits. Obesity, diabetes, and heart disease are hitting the population like never before. There's a compound effect to bad habits, too. Deferred gratification can help combat those bad habits. I'm living proof that good habits, compound effect, and deferred gratification works. I'm 55 years old, I can run 40-70 miles a week, I last took a Tylenol three years ago, I haven't been sick in six years, I'm at a healthy weight, I sleep well, I haven't been injured in 30 years of running, my cognitive skills are quick, I have an upbeat outlook on life, and I want others to have the same thing.

Another habit I implement in my life for a positive outlook is that I pray/meditate every morning. I want and need to get my mind right for the day before I go for my run. When I pray/meditate, it sets the stage for the day. I ask God to help me be better than I was the day before so I can be used to help other people do the same. I try to look introspectively and commit myself to doing my best every day. I am not always successful, I am a work in progress, but more times than not, I'm on point. I want to be there for other people. I want to exude both humility and confidence, along with appreciation and gratitude every day.

I strive to be emotionally unshakeable. The important thing is to remain committed to being intentional in living up to your potential. That doesn't come by chance, but by choice: Your choice! If you want to climb to the top of a high mountain, it's going to take work and you will have to make a decision to climb it. When you get to the top of the mountain you will feel great that you reached your goal and then look for the next goal to achieve. However, you can also make a decision to do nothing and stay at the bottom of the mountain. That will take no effort at all to stay there. I challenge you today to make a choice to start setting goals for you to achieve. It will build strength and character within you.

Sometimes, despite our best efforts, we may hit a speed bump where we don't see a lot of results. We have all experienced diminishing returns. When this happens, it may be time to course correct. We're not trees, we can actually change and move. One of my strategies I use to help navigate a possible change in the direction I'm going involves reading books on the subject until I find a plan that works for me. When you're looking for a teacher, one usually appears, which simply means that there are teachers all around us. Often, we won't notice them until we're looking for one. Be around others that inspire you to be a better version of yourself. If you're experiencing diminishing returns, get around those who you admire and respect and they will help you; the types of people you wouldn't mind trading places with—role models. Get away from people who don't aspire to live their best life and get around people who do, and this will help you elevate your thinking and your life.

Having a mentor is helpful to have a positive life. At the time I didn't see it, but I had a mentor in the sheriff's department when I was coming up the ranks. He was the assistant director and a great runner. I have always been very fortunate to meet good people. People have generally looked out for me. Where I'm at in life is because other people have helped me to get here.

Overall, no matter what you do to positively change your life, change takes time. There were many things that I was either afraid to do or was told I couldn't do, but I have done and continue to do them. But it took time to get me to that point. I was the least athletic person in my family then I became one of the most athletic in my family through my running. I had never traveled much before, and now I have traveled the world. I was one of the least likely people in my family to have chosen a career in law enforcement and now after a nearly 30-year law enforcement career, I retired as a lieutenant at the sheriff's department. I have made it a habit to habit stack my life, which simply means one good habit after another. That was a component of what my early life was missing. I'm now a more fulfilled person than I have ever been. I am driven by my purpose, which is to serve God by being everything that He has created me to be.

12

GENEROSITY

One of the best feelings in the world is giving. The positive energy is contagious. With just one act of kindness, you can inspire others to go out and do the same. I go back to Albert Einstein because he said it's every person's "obligation to put back into the world at least the equivalent of what that person takes out of it." Take my Aunt Mary (my dad's youngest sister) and my Uncle Nick as perfect examples. They were an integral part of my success. They have been there to help me in my time of need and supported me in my goals and dreams. I'm a lot like my Aunt Mary. We both have Type A personalities. We both make it a habit to consistently work out, are motivated, and purpose-driven. She told me even though I was retiring (which happened in July of 2021), she knew I would never be retired. She will never fully retire either. My aunt and I are kindred spirits. She doesn't settle for a mediocre life. She believes that you should live your best life, and take care of yourself, spiritually, physically, emotionally, mentally, and financially. We always push to be our best. She and my uncle have always shown their love for our entire family by opening up their house to us. They always invite the whole family over to their house for Thanksgiving and Christmas feasts with nothing asked in return. They help keep our family together. They have always encouraged me to keep my faith and they always pray for me. After my marriage to Lynn fell apart, I was so broken up over it. I felt that I was in actual physical pain and I didn't know what to do and where to turn. I went to my Aunt Mary and Uncle Nick, and they were there for me. There was never any judgement.

My aunt and uncle are also very generous and give their time and resources without expecting anything in return. Two examples of my aunt's and uncle's generosity stand out. The first example happened 30 years ago, just before I got my job at the sheriff's department. I told my aunt I was going to take the family to Disneyland, and she wrote me a check for three hundred dollars and said "I just want to give you this so you can spend an extra day at Disneyland." My jaw dropped. In today's money that would probably amount to $1,000 dollars. Another example of their generosity happened when things had just started to get bumpy between Lynn and I, and I decided it would be a good thing to take her and the kids on an overnight road trip a couple hours away from our house. We stayed in a motel that wasn't on the best side of the town we were in, that's for sure. In the morning I got up to pack up our belongings in the car.

I couldn't believe that all four tires on my car were flat. The parking at the motel was full, but my car was the only one in the lot whose tires had been slashed. I didn't know what to do. I had no money. I called Aunt Mary and told her what had happened. She said, "Don't worry, stay there. Uncle Nick will be on his way right now." My uncle drove over two hours away to help me with no questions asked. He called a tow truck to have my car towed to the nearest tire shop and bought me four new tires and said not to worry about paying him back right away, just pay him when I had the money. That day he spent at least six hours of his day (the round trip of travel plus two hours to help me while he was there) to help a stranded nephew out. I will never forget how much they did for me. That act of kindness and generosity impacted me that day. I'm hoping to impact others through kindness and generosity also through various means. Often, when people are going through a difficult time in their life, they just need to know that they matter and people really do care about them. A simple act of kindness or generosity can go a long way in helping people get out of a bad place in life. My aunt and uncle never judged me even though she knew I wasn't doing my best as a youngster. Aunt Mary would say things like, "I know you can do better and I'm always here for you."

I'm here to tell you, it's better to give than to receive and love in such a way that others can feel it just being around you. The more I've given, the more I have received, and I'm talking about kindness and generosity much more than I'm talking about money. You don't know who you're affecting when you simply say, "Have a nice day." Give more than you're getting, and you will get far in life. That is one of the purposes of me writing this book: to give back. I participate in the Latino Role Model Conference once a year. I go into the areas of San Jose considered to be a bit rough and I encourage the kids that attend the conference that they, too, can achieve anything they put their minds to. I want to show others that if you do certain things, like positive, productive daily habits, this will compound and will add up to having success in the area of their choosing. It's like putting money into an investment account, and over time that money will add up by compounding interest. I want to show that I'm living proof this works! Adam went from a kid who wasn't displaying good healthy habits to an adult who pushes hard to succeed. I want to get others in the right mindset that will help take them up to the level of their dreams.

CONCLUSION

My dad's religious turnaround was an overnight change in his life. He made a decision and stuck with it. Eventually, I did the same thing he did by accepting God into my life, which gave me a definitive sense of purpose. I changed my environment and changed my associations and this changed my life. My faith pulled me through some rough times. This book is not meant to preach to anyone, but to show you what helped me in my journey and my belief is that it can help you too . I leaned back on my faith. But faith without action is dead. You can say "I love you," but if you show no action behind the words, it means nothing. It's hollow. You have to participate in your own rescue if you want a more fulfilled life. You should live healthy physically, mentally, and spiritually. Be mindful to always be mindful. As far as priorities go, we should always know that "the most important thing is that we keep the most important thing, the most important thing in our lives." That last sentence refers to the importance of having priorities in life.. Live with gratitude, thankfulness, and appreciation daily.

It all boils down to this: you can achieve anything if you have a strong enough purpose. The message can be transformative if you employ certain habits. To review:

1. It's not where you start, it's where you end up that matters. We tend to have the belief that we are only a product of our family and neighborhood environment. In some ways that is true, but we have the power to change the outcome of that. It's not so much what has happened to us, but rather how we respond to what has happened to us. We need to take full responsibility for where we are in life, and where we are not. If we do take responsibility for our life, then we have the power to change our life. Get around people who you admire and want to model yourself after. If you do that, you will begin to feel that it's possible and attainable for you. Venture out of your comfort zone and try it for yourself. I came from what some people would call the "wrong side of the tracks" and I was a troubled youth, yet ended up having a successful career. I worked in law enforcement for almost 30 years, ultimately becoming a lieutenant for the sheriff's department, and I helped manage about 170 officers until I retired.

2. Develop a plan to gain the ability of being comfortable with being uncomfortable, and of trying new things, and trying things to find purpose in.

3. Where you want to go in life depends on associations that either help or hinder you getting there. Without good associations, over time, it's very difficult to achieve success, and you may settle for mediocrity and then try to use logic

and reason to justify yourself. You may start thinking that life isn't so bad, when you know very well that you could be doing much better. No parent wants to hear that their child is doing average or below average on their grades when you know they can do better. How are we doing in our adult life? Are we making the grade? Or are we average, below average, or even failing? Well, if you are not making the grade, please don't rationalize why you aren't. The great news is you can start to turn it around today! Start by getting around others who are already making the grade. If you get off track, you can get back on track. Get around others who are crushing their goals, and soon you will begin crushing your goals as well.

4. Be positive. Be around positive people. Cut down on watching the negative news cycle. Garbage in is garbage out. Be careful what you look at and be careful what you hear. It can affect your happiness.

5. If you're not feeling your best physically, you can never be your best overall. Stay active! Be mindful of what you put into your body. If you eat a bunch of garbage and sweets, you will feel like garbage. Live a cleaner, healthier lifestyle and you'll begin to feel better in every way. If you do an exercise that elevates your heart rate for a sustained period of time, such as running, you will feel better, and your thought process will change. In his book '*Spark*,' Dr. John

Ratey cites an October 2000 study out of Duke University which concluded that exercise is better than Zoloft in treating depression. He further states that if exercise came in a pill form, it would be hailed as the blockbuster drug of the century. Therefore, get out there and get your body moving!

6. Thought-to-action has followed me for a long time, even though I wasn't able to articulate that principle, my friend and mentor Evan Carmichael who is a global social media sensation explained it to me. I used to just hang out and not see plans for the future. Broken people hanging around other broken people don't get healed. You have to remove yourself from people who don't add value to your life. Loyalty to broken people will only keep you broken. Once again, you have to participate in your own rescue. You have to remove yourself from other people that don't serve your best interests.

7. Don't beat yourself up. Do something every day that helps you move forward towards your goal. Writing down simple daily goals can help keep you on point. I don't give up these days even though I was once called a quitter. Baby steps and good habits pay off over time.

I truly believe that living life on purpose, which means you have to be intentional, is an essential element to attaining goals. Anyone can do it if they have faith and are willing to take action in their journey. We all have to recognize that associations matter, environment matters, mindset matters, reading matters, exercise matters, healthy eating habits matter. In other words, Everything you do and think matters! Don't just settle but try new things, so you can maintain the mindset of doing uncomfortable things. This has helped me to not be afraid to challenge myself. I stay comfortable with being uncomfortable. I push myself to stay disciplined with exercise, meditation, prayer, and reading. Warren Buffet said, "Skip a daily meal but not your daily reading." Leaders are readers. I fill my mind with resources and tools that help me stay on point in attaining my goals. In his book, 'Make Your Bed,' retired Admiral William H. McRaven recommends fixing your bed every morning. It sounds kind of goofy at first, but if you do that, you start the day with a win by being disciplined. I start the day with being accomplished. I also go out on a run five days a week, then I come home and take a cold shower and then I read. I self-reflect at the end of each day to see if I did my very best. Did I do more than what's expected of me? Did I exude appreciation and gratitude and thankfulness to people in my life? Did I do more for others? This is my mindset.

I have been fortunate enough to have traveled the world, and what I've noticed is that in spite of their governments, good or bad, people generally just want to be happy and want to live in peace. People may look different from us, have a different culture, speak a different language, and observe different religions in different time zones, but we're all looking for the same thing. We all want peace, love, happiness, and a sense of fulfillment in our lives. I have found that in my faith and then being intentional about living the life I was designed to live.

I saw it time and time again during my law enforcement career. People come out of jail, and they all say they want to do good. What happens is as long as things are going their way, they seem motivated. But when life happens and challenging times hit them, many revert to unhealthy bad habits they've previously known. My goal is that this book will inspire people to stay positive, motivated, and inspired to not just survive but thrive in spite of life's challenges. It's through the challenges that we gain strength and growth. Life happens for us, not to us. If people feed on negativity and have a dark view of life, it's hard to advance. You need belief in yourself to improve. A positive outlook on life is a key ingredient to living a happy and successful life. Your Self Talk and being Self Aware are huge ingredients to success.

I hope my story informs people that it doesn't matter where you came from, you can learn to be inspired and disciplined and "Live Life on Purpose." Live your best life! Become your best self that you can be and don't accept living a life that is less than the life you were born to live. I'm not saying it's easy to attain, but I am saying it is possible. It starts with a belief in something bigger than yourself. That you are not here by accident, but by divine design. There has never been or ever will be a person just like you in the world! That means that you are one of a kind! You are Priceless! Once you comprehend that, you will be on your way to living a life of fulfillment. It starts with realizing how very special and valuable you are! Don't wait any longer to begin! You got this!

It's important to note that although it may seem scary to be around new things or a different crowd, PLEASE STICK WITH IT! I promise you that the feeling is only temporary. Before you know it, you will start to change/transform into the person you want to be, and those who think like you or like what you're doing will gravitate towards you like a magnet. Then you will be around people who have similar goals and mindsets. They will add value to your life, and you to theirs. It won't feel uncomfortable anymore, however it will create momentum and now you will start to wonder what else you can achieve. This will mean you will be uncomfortable again, but once again only for a short time. This is where you really start to believe in yourself and understand that you are LIMITLESS and there is nothing that you can't do!

Inch by inch it's a cinch, but yard by yard it's hard. You don't need to take giant steps. Just do a little something every day that moves you forward in the direction of your goals. It's just like compound interest, if you daily put in a little something, over time you will be amazed at your progress.

You've got to believe in yourself and your God-given gifts and capabilities more than you believe in anybody else, because if you believe in yourself, you are limitless. Ceilings are made by us so they can be broken by us. Although, I do believe we all want to be happy and succeed, there is a Ralph Waldo Emerson quote which says, "The purpose in life is not to be happy. It's to be useful, to be honorable, to be compassionate, to have it make a difference that you have lived and lived well."

I know where I've come from, and believe me, if I can succeed in living with purpose and living well, you can too! You matter! You are loved and don't ever forget that you truly are Limitless!!

ACKNOWLEDGEMENTS:

When I first had the idea to write this book, I had no idea how to begin or even to know the amount of time and work it would take. I soon realized that it would take a team effort to bring this book into reality. First thing I did was pose the idea to those closest to me, whom I respected. I want to thank my good friend and running buddy Juan, who is actually more like my brother, who encouraged and supported me and helped me get this book from just an idea I had to its completion. I want to thank my cousin Tommy for his constant help/ insight and belief in me to bring this book into a reality. I want to thank Lynette for her support and recommendations after reading the first draft of the book. Juan, Tommy, and Lynette all read the first rough draft and offered valuable suggestions on how to make the book even better and more impactful. I would like to give a special thank you to Laura, who when I first brought up the idea to write this book and asked if she would like to be a part of it, and without hesitation gave a resounding "Yes, of course, I would like to be a part of it." Laura, because of your love for God and people, you from the beginning of this project have put in countless hours along with your heart and soul to make this book a success.

You helped keep me focused and paid attention to the details needed to assure this book would help all who read it find their purpose and live up to their God-given potential. Last but certainly not least, I would like to thank all the readers who took the time to read my book. My goal was to share my story in the hope that you will Live Your Life on Purpose as I have learned and am still learning. I now would like to thank the Lord for not only giving me the ability to write this book, but also the desire to write it.

Made in the USA
Las Vegas, NV
10 September 2022